The life of The Beatles

We are the Beatles: John Lennon, Paul McCartney, George Harrison, and Ringo Starr. We all grew up in Liverpool, England, in the 1940s and '50s, after the Second World War. Times were hard, and the city was very rundown; there was rationing and high unemployment. Little did we know how things would change politically, socially, and culturally in the

Illustrations by Leanne Goodall.

Text by Claire Sipi.

Designed by Nick Ackland.

White Star Kids™ is a trademark of White Star s.r.l.

© 2023 White Star s.r.l.
Piazzale Luigi Cadorna, 6
20123 Milan, Italy
www.whitestar.it

Produced by I am a bookworm.

Editing: Michele Suchomel-Casey

First printing August 2023

ISBN 978-88-544-2010-6
1 2 3 4 5 6   27 26 25 24 23

Printed in China by Dream Colour (Hong Kong) Printing Limited

revolutionary 1960s and how we would be a major part of this change. Come with us as we share our incredible journey, from being four inexperienced musicians playing gigs at local venues in our home city to becoming international rock stars and one of the most successful and influential bands in the history of popular music.

John Lennon

Julia

Alfred

John

I was born on October 9, 1940, in Liverpool, England. I lived in a tiny
house with my mum, Julia, and my grandparents. My dad, Alfred, worked
on a ship and was away for months at a time. After a while he stopped
sending money and eventually didn't come home at all. Things were
hard for my mum, and she decided it would be best for me if I went
to live with my Aunt Mimi.

I was a happy boy, and I still saw my mum regularly. My aunt tried to encourage me to study hard, but as I grew older the only thing I was interested in was art and music. My mum bought me a guitar and taught me how to play it. I loved the new rock and roll music that was coming out of America. Elvis Presley was my hero, and I wanted to play the guitar like him. I formed my own band at school, called the Quarrymen.

Just before my 18th birthday, my mum was hit by a car and killed. I was devastated, and this had a profound effect on my life and my music.

Paul McCartney

Michael

Mary

Jim

Paul

I was born on June 18, 1942, in Liverpool. I had a happy home life with my
younger brother, Michael, my mum, Mary, who was a nurse, and my dad,
Jim. I worked hard at school, and I loved writing, drawing, and music. My dad
was a great musical influence on me. In his spare time, he played the piano,
and he and his brother formed a group called Jim Mac's Jazz Band.

My musical rock and roll heroes were Little Richard and Elvis Presley. I loved the way they played, sang, and danced onstage. I really wanted to be like them! I taught myself the guitar, and I tried to copy Little Richard's style of loud scream-like singing.

Sadly, when I was 14, my mum died from cancer. Music became everything to me as I tried to deal with my sadness.

George Harrison

I was born on February 25, 1943, in Liverpool, the youngest of four children. My dad, Harold, drove a bus, and my mum, Louise, taught ballroom dancing. I was a quiet but happy child in a busy, loving home.

I didn't really get into music until I was a teenager, when I heard a new type of music called skiffle, which was a mixture of jazz, blues, and American folk sounds. I begged my mum to buy me a guitar so that I could learn to play this exciting music like some of my favorite guitar heroes, Django Reinhardt and Lonnie Donegan. Later, when I heard Elvis Presley's music, I started playing rock and roll, too.

I practiced and practiced until I got good enough to form my own band with one of my brothers. We were called the Rebels. I loved playing the guitar, and I knew I wanted to pursue a career in music.

Ringo Starr

I was born on July 7, 1940, in Liverpool, the only child of Elsie and Richard Starkey. I was named Richard, after my dad, but I changed my name to Ringo Starr when I became a musician. My dad left when I was three, and I was a lonely, sickly child. I missed a lot of school because of illness and truancy, and I fell behind in my studies. Then, when I was 13, I became ill with tuberculosis and had to spend two years in a children's hospital.

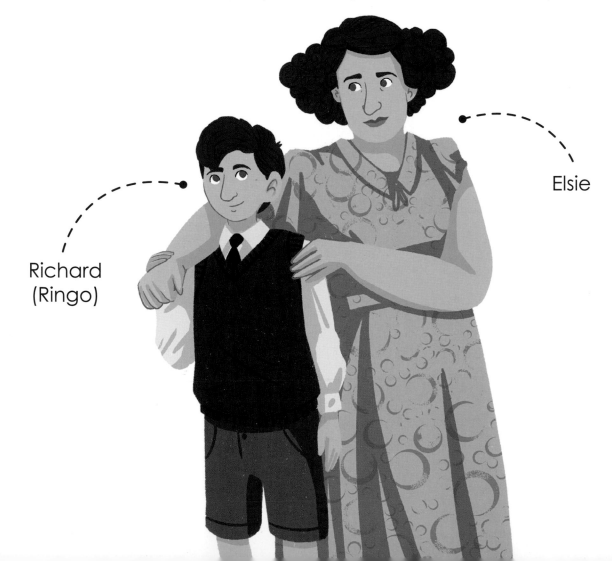

Richard
(Ringo)

Elsie

It was during this time that my lifelong passion for drumming was born. The hospital had a band that played to cheer up the patients. I would bang along to the music on my bedside cabinet. When I finally returned home, I made my own set of drums out of old pots and practiced all the time.

I left school at 15 and had a lot of different jobs. I formed a band with some of my work colleagues, and when I got my first real drum kit in 1957, we started doing local gigs. A few years later I joined a successful skiffle group, Rory Storm and the Hurricanes. We were offered work in Hamburg, Germany, and this is where I first met the other members of the Beatles.

Rock and roll music emerged in the early 1950s, with its roots and upbeat sounds coming from the exciting rhythm and blues (R&B) music developed by Black Americans in the 1940s in America.

Parts of America at that time were segregated, and people of color weren't allowed to mix with white people. They were not treated fairly or given the same rights or opportunities as whites. Radio DJs wouldn't play the R&B music of Black artists on their shows, and as young boys growing up in England, we didn't know this music even existed. It wasn't until music producers got popular white artists, like Elvis Presley, to perform the R&B music of Black artists, like Little Richard and Fats Domino, that this "forbidden" music was allowed to be broadcast on the radio. Rock and roll was born!

The fast, jazzy beats of rock and roll and the use of electric guitars, the double bass, drum sets, and loud piano melodies was very different from the music that our parents had listened to. It was considered quite shocking at the time. As teenagers we loved it because we could sing and dance along to it and because culturally and politically it went against everything our parents' generation believed in. It was against this exciting musical backdrop that we started to come together as a band.

John and Paul met at one of the Quarrymen's gigs in the summer of 1957. John invited Paul to join the band as rhythm guitarist. Paul already new George from school and arranged for him to audition for John. John was impressed with George's guitar playing and invited him to join the band, too. John asked his art school friend Stuart Sutcliffe to play bass guitar, even though Stuart didn't know how to play the instrument at first! Ringo didn't join the band until 1962. Before him, several drummers came and went.

At first, we performed as the Quarrymen at local gigs in Liverpool. By 1960, after several band name changes, we finally decided to call ourselves the Beatles, as a tribute to Buddy Holly's band, the Crickets, and the popular British "Beat" music of the time. It was as the Beatles that we auditioned for and won a 48-night residency gig in Hamburg, Germany. We needed a drummer to complete our lineup, and we asked Pete Best, another Liverpool lad, to join us.

Not yet knowing what lay in store for us, we set off on our new adventure to Hamburg. Our families weren't very happy, but we were determined to make a go of it. This was our first steady paying job, and we were excited.

The club in Hamburg where we performed, the Indra, wasn't exactly what we had been promised by the club owner! It was a dirty, rundown place, and we had to use the public toilet as our dressing room. Our accommodation was a small room behind the screen at a local movie theater. We were expected to perform at the club for eight hours at a time, and quite often fights broke out among drunken fans in the audience. We worked hard, but we were tired and hungry much of the time.

One benefit of playing for such long hours was that we all improved musically, and we became more popular in Germany and at home. John and Paul were writing loads of songs for us. We did another Hamburg residency in 1961, and one more in 1962. Stuart decided to leave the band in the summer of 1961, so Paul took up the bass guitar in his place. Tragically, Stuart died in 1962 of a brain hemorrhage.

Back in Liverpool, between the Hamburg gigs, bigger clubs like the Cavern started asking us to perform. It was during this time that we met Brian Epstein, a music columnist and record store owner. He loved our sound and could see our potential. We signed him as our band manager at the end of 1961.

One of the first things Brian did was improve our image. Gone were the scruffy lads in leather jackets, with greased-back hair; we now wore matching suits and ties onstage and styled our hair brushed forward. Our hairstyle became known as the Beatle mop top.

After our Hamburg residency in 1962, Brian got us released from the contract with the club owner, and he signed a recording contract for us with EMI's Parlophone label, with the producer George Martin. He also fired Pete. We felt bad because Pete was our friend, but we didn't think he really fit in with the band. We asked Ringo Starr to be our drummer. With this new lineup, the four of us would go on to become a world-famous band.

From that point on, things happened very fast. We released our first single, "Love Me Do," toward the end of 1962, and our second single, "Please Please Me," in January 1963, which went to number one on the British charts. We also released two chart-topping albums in 1963, *Please Please Me* and *With the Beatles*, followed by a string of successful singles and albums over the next few years.

THE BEATLES!

Suddenly we were stars, doing UK tours and earning lots of money. Our gigs sold out, and our fans copied our fashion style and chased us wherever we went. We attracted a lot of media interest in the UK, with newspapers calling us the Fab Four. The excitement and hysteria of our screaming fans came to be dubbed Beatlemania.

It wasn't until 1964, however, that we started attracting attention in the United States. At first the critics didn't like us, but after a TV appearance on *The Ed Sullivan Show*, and once Brian secured us a recording deal with Capitol Records (EMI's American subsidiary company), Beatlemania hit the United States and we were truly world-famous rock stars!

Tours, hit singles and albums, media appearances, and films followed. We were the heroes of the rock and pop world and icons for the hopes and dreams of the revolutionary 1960s. The incredible attention we received paved the way for other British bands, like the Kinks and the Rolling Stones, to break into the American music scene. The newspapers called this phenomenon the British Invasion.

It was an incredible time for us, but we hadn't realized just how much being rock stars would affect our personal lives. We were exhausted, and there was very little time to rest or be with our families, between the back-to-back concert tours, media interviews, film-making, and grueling recording sessions.

Fame comes with a price. We had so many screaming fans at our concerts that we couldn't hear ourselves playing or singing our music, and we could never be alone. Wherever we went, even in our private time, our fans followed us.

We were tired of all the traveling and attention, and we wanted to spend more time writing songs and developing our music. Under all this pressure, cracks began to appear in our relationships with each other.

Eventually, in 1966, despite our manager's reservations about us doing it, we decided to stop touring and performing. We returned home to focus on our music and recording, and to spend time with our families.

The world of the 1960s was a very different place to that of the 1950s. People were angry about a lot of social and political issues, like segregation and the Vietnam War. They were protesting in the streets, calling for change. Musicians were reflecting these feelings in their songs, and we wanted to do the same.

For the next few years our music mirrored the revolutionary times we lived in. We experimented with protest lyrics and different genres of music, introducing classical and folk elements and using instruments and melodies from Indian music.

Despite our musical success during the last years of the 1960s, our personal differences caused us to drift apart. We tried to keep up a public appearance of togetherness in our music and produced some of our most successful works, like *Sgt. Pepper's Lonely Hearts Club Band*, but behind the scenes the band was disintegrating.

The sudden death of our manager, Brian, in 1967, left us in chaos, and it was the beginning of the end for us as a band. We decided to manage ourselves. Ongoing disagreements and a string of bad business decisions over the next few years finally tore us apart. As a band we had symbolized the dreams of a generation; individually we had succumbed to the pressures of fame and couldn't live up to that ideal anymore. It was 1970 and the Beatles were over.

After our breakup, we all went on to have solo musical careers. Individually, we used our status as rock stars to try and make the world a better place, with various protests and charitable endeavors.

Tragically, in 1980, John was assassinated by a crazed fan. Family, friends, and fans around the world were devastated. Then sadly in 2001, George died from cancer. Both George and John are celebrated and missed by their families and friends and remembered by the world for their contribution to music. Paul and Ringo still make music, much to fans' delight.

The Beatles may be no more, but our impact on the musical culture of the 1960s is written in history, and our still-popular songs will be listened to by generations to come. The legacy of our music continues with many artists taking inspiration from our hits.

On July 7, Ringo Starr is born. On October 9, John Lennon is born.

February 25: George Harrison is born.

The band changes its name to the Beatles. They play in Hamburg, Germany, under their new name.

1940

1943

1960

1942

1956

June 18: Paul McCartney is born.

John forms his first band, the Quarrymen.

Ringo Starr becomes the band's drummer. The band records their first song, "Love Me Do."

The Beatles perform their biggest concert, to 55,000 fans, at Shea Stadium, in New York City.

1962

1965

1961

1963

1967

Brian Epstein becomes their manager after seeing the Beatles perform at the Cavern in Liverpool.

The Beatles' manager, Brian Epstein, dies on the August 27.

Second single, "Please Please Me," becomes their first number one hit.

On December 8, John
is assassinated in
New York by a fan.

On January 30, the
Beatles give their last live
performance together,
in the rooftop garden
of their office.

The Beatles get a
star on Hollywood's
Walk of Fame.

1969

1980

1998

1970

1994

Last recording session
at Abbey Road Studios.
Paul officially announces
the breakup of the Beatles.

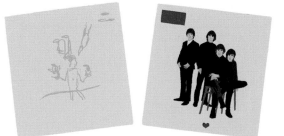

In tribute to John, the remaining
Beatles, George, Paul, and Ringo,
work together on two new
Beatles' songs, "Free as a Bird"
and "Real Love," both written
and recorded as demos by John.

Paul and Ringo reunite for a benefit concert. Digitally remastered CDs of the entire Beatles' catalog are released.

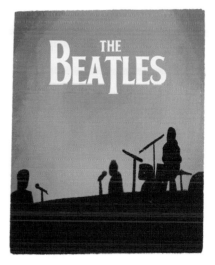

Peter Jackson's documentary, *The Beatles: Get Back*, is released.

2009

2021

2001

2014

2023

The Beatles win the Lifetime Achievement Award at the Grammys.

On November 29, George dies of cancer. Shortly after his death, a memorial tree is planted for him in Los Angeles.

Paul and Ringo are still performing live concerts.

QUESTIONS

Q1. Can you name the four Beatles?

Q2. Where did the Beatles grow up?

Q3. What was the name of John's first band,
which later became the Beatles?

Q4. What genre of music did rock and roll evolve from?

Q5. Where did the Beatles get their first
steady paying work?

Q6. What was the Beatles' fan hysteria called by the press?

Q7. The Beatles led the way for other British bands to break into the American music scene. What was this phenomenon called?

Q8. Who were the Beatles' manager and record producer?

Q9. When did the Beatles stop touring and doing concerts?

Q10. Name the Beatles' first single and their last album.

ANSWERS

A1. John Lennon, Paul McCartney, George Harrison, and Ringo Starr.

A2. Liverpool, England.

A3. The Quarrymen.

A4. Rhythm and blues (R&B).

A5. The Indra Club in Hamburg, Germany.

A6. Beatlemania.

A7. The British Invasion.

A8. Brian Epstein and George Martin.

A9. 1966.

A10. First single: "Love Me Do" (1962); first album: "Please Please Me" (1963).